Loneliness

 caring for yourself and others

Loneliness

🕊 caring for yourself and others

Christine Olsen

Published by Redemptorist Publications
Alphonsus House, Chawton, Hampshire, GU34 3HQ, UK
Tel: +44 (0)1420 88222, Fax. +44 (0)1420 88805
Email: rp@rpbooks.co.uk, www.rpbooks.co.uk

A registered charity limited by guarantee
Registered in England 3261721

Copyright © Redemptorist Publications 2017
First published November 2017

Series Editor: Sr Janet Fearns
Edited by Bahram Francis Rafat
Designed by Eliana Thompson

ISBN 978-0-85231-505-7

A CIP catalogue record for this book is available from the British Library.

The author would like to thank all those who have also contributed to this book with the
true stories written in their own words.

The publisher gratefully acknowledges permission to use the following copyright material:
Excerpts from the *New Revised Standard Version Bible*: Anglicized Edition, copyright © 1989,
1995 National Council of the Churches of Christ in the United States of America. Used by
permission. All rights reserved.

Excerpt from the *New King James Version*®. Copyright © 1982 by Thomas Nelson.
Used by permission. All rights reserved.

The publisher gratefully acknowledges permission to use the poems of Carol Pallett
and the poems authored anonymously. "Endless Silence"; "Another Day" © Carol Pallett.

Printed by Lithgo Press Ltd.,
Leicester, LE8 6NU

Introduction   1

1. Please listen   3

2. Working in the community to reduce
   loneliness and social isolation   5

3. Asset Based Community Development   9

4. Loneliness within our churches   15

5. Loneliness and vulnerability   23

6. You can change the future   29

7. The old has gone, the new is on its way   33

8. Prayer   37

9. True stories   47

10. Some poems from the heart about loneliness   57

Web resources   62

Introduction

Loneliness is not the same as being alone.

One can be alone and perfectly content, relishing the silence, enjoying the space.

No, loneliness is not just about being alone.

Loneliness is that empty space that fills you with longing, yearning for someone to come and fill it, someone who cares.

Loneliness can afflict any of us at any stage in our lives be it the loneliness of the friendless child on the playground or the devastation of losing your partner of sixty years and having to face your remaining days so very alone.

Loneliness can strike anyone, anywhere. It could be

* your colleague at work, bullied and ground down by the boss
* your son or daughter, bullied on the bus to school
* your friend whose husband ran off with a younger woman
* your mate whose wife was hit by a bus
* your mum who cannot see her way to living without your dad
* your neighbour, struggling to still find his wife in her dementia

It is devastating when it hits.

I wish I could say that this book will provide all the answers. It can't. However, in sharing other people's experiences of loneliness it might be of help.

Seeing folk who are worse off than yourself doesn't necessarily help but I believe that knowing that others suffer similar pain can bring a strange comfort. My hope and that of those who have generously contributed their experience to this book, is that its readers will recognise a companion in the abyss of loneliness. Others have experienced it and have come through it. You can too.

1

Please listen

"I live alone and fear I am losing the ability to speak. Please listen to me – and thank you for listening."

Have you ever met someone at the bus stop, someone who says something nondescript about the weather and, the next thing you know, you have heard their life story?

Ever wondered why that might be? Imagine living alone without a living thing in your home. How good must it feel to be able to use your voice; to have someone listen and be concerned about you and your life. That priceless gift is so easy to give. All it takes is that you control the urge to give advice or to tell your own equally fascinating story. When out with our friends we expect to give and take in the conversation, but when visiting a housebound lady or gent, be gracious and allow them to be the giver. Stop, listen and receive. You will do more good than you can possibly imagine. You will also have the opportunity to learn so much about someone's life and loves.

I periodically visit a gentleman who is in his nineties. He makes me a cup of coffee and I settle down for a good chat. This involves letting him speak, interrupting only to clarify a detail or show that I am still engaged. He is a great storyteller and the hour flies past. I feel so privileged to hear this local history from one who was there. These are times to treasure for when those in their nineties die, their life stories go with them. As I leave he always compliments me on being such a good listener. "When my neighbour listens he always interrupts so I lose the thread of my story," he says. "Then I can't remember where I got to and he always wants to tell me what I should do. I don't want him to tell me what I should do. I know what I should do."

This is good advice.

How can I help?

- How are my listening skills?

- Do I offer solutions before someone has finished speaking?

- Who are the good listeners in this parish?

- How can we engage their skills?

2

Working in the community to reduce loneliness and social isolation

I work for a lottery-funded project called Ageing Well, one of fourteen UK projects set up to tackle the growing problem of loneliness in our society. My job description is "Community Builder".

Where I live in Devon is a well-known beauty spot where many people choose to retire, giving us an above average percentage of older citizens. As active sixty-year-olds, they move here to the bungalows above the town, seduced by the wonderful vistas stretching down to the sea. Who wouldn't want to live in such a place? While they can drive, these are good properties and they have a comfortable life. Many bungalows are detached with a large garden. Moving here from an overcrowded city to a very affordable home must feel like a dream come true. But twenty years down the line, now in their eighties, we find people who struggle with poor vision due to macular degeneration and/or cataracts. They struggle with mobility due to arthritis in hands, feet, knees and backs. Some live with constant pain due to fibromyalgia and a host of other health issues.

Suddenly the large open space around their homes is less attractive. They wish they had neighbours who might pop in. They wish they could reach the bus. Some, after fifty or sixty years of happy marriage, now have to cope with the devastating loss of their lifelong partner. At the same time, they are losing their longstanding friends, brothers and sisters. Life no longer looks quite so good.

This is the context in which I am working. However, we operate in a different way to the norm. We do not go out looking for problems. Rather we seek the solutions that are there if one has the eyes to see them. We look for spaces where people can and do get together. We identify groups of like-minded people who share common interests. Most of all, we look for the people who are natural connectors. You know the sort: you are probably one of them if you are reading this book as a pastoral worker. Natural connectors are those people who love to bring people together. They do not expect a networking reward. They just enjoy helping people make new positive relationships.

Natural connectors can be found chatting to the person next to them at the bus stop, or waiting at the doctor's. They might be making time pass quicker in the queue at the supermarket or enlivening a dull train journey. Natural connectors have a harder time today than they did in the past, not because they have changed but because the world in which they live is changing. People are connected to their phones much of the time when they are waiting. Those gaps in which connections could be made are being plugged by machines. Don't hear me wrong: I am delighted that I can make a quick call while I walk to my next appointment. But if I do, I will miss an unrepeatable opportunity to speak to someone who is actually there in front of me.

My life as a Community Builder is fluid. I go where the energy is. A member of the community must have requested anything that I help to set up. I write a monthly article in our local community magazine. In it I talk about groups I have visited and people I have met. I always end by asking people to get in touch if they have an idea that they would like to make happen or if they know someone who may be lonely or isolated. I won't meet many lonely, isolated people in the groups I visit but I will bump into people who know of them.

I would love to see churches take on this mission within their communities. It is the nature of a Christian to want to take Christ's love out into the world. If each person in any given church community would take responsibility for lessening the loneliness of one other person, we would transform our neighbourhoods.

I spoke to a lady who lives in a new block of retirement flats and suggested that, with eighty apartments, there was no need for anyone to be lonely. They have people all around them without needing to leave the building. I thought that this lovely, friendly Christian woman would jump at the opportunity to lessen the loneliness of others. Instead, she said that she would be afraid lest one of these lonely residents should latch on to her and outstay their welcome; that she would be lumbered by someone's neediness; that her home would be compromised and no longer feel a safe place to be. We need to shift that perspective. By closing the door "in case I meet the wrong sort", I also close the door to opportunities for very real and valuable friendships, ones that might alleviate my own loneliness as well as theirs.

How can I help?

- What organisations or facilities are there in this area which can help people to feel needed, valued and less lonely?

- What can I do to help people to feel valued?

This is the mission field. This is my journey and yours. How do we close the gap so that people can keep safe boundaries, maintaining control over their homes but also creating doorways and gates through which they might meet each other?

"Loneliness and the feeling of being unwanted is the most terrible poverty."

St Teresa of Calcutta

3

Asset Based Community Development

> "I like to listen. I have learned a great deal from listening carefully. Most people never listen."

> *Ernest Hemingway*

The Ageing Well project is using a new model called Asset Based Community Development or ABCD. This model does what it says in the title. A team of Community Builders, each responsible for a different area, map the assets that are to be found in their area. Assets are many and various and need creative eyes to recognise them.

Some assets are physical places. Community centres, churches and more importantly their halls host a multitude of groups, as do the public swimming pool, parks, beaches, recreation grounds and playing fields. Shops, large and small, cafes and restaurants, doctors' surgeries, pharmacies, pubs and private clubs are all "bumping spaces" where a Community Builder can "bump into people" and have conversations.

Every conversation holds out possibilities. For example, one day, in the supermarket buying vegetables, I bumped into a friend who was in the choir to which I used to belong. She reminded me that, with mixed feelings, she would soon retire from her much-loved work with the nearby Depression and Anxiety Service (DAS). Her words sparked the seed of an idea. DAS already sends people to my groups for help with reintegrating people into the community. What if she were to use her DAS connections? Could we set up a group to help people make that an easier transition over a longer period than current DAS funding allows?

Sometimes my conversation is with a group. Here, there are different possibilities. I tell them what I am trying to do, how I want to help their group to flourish and how they in their turn can help ease people into their group. If group members are willing to give me their contact details I contact them if I meet someone who might benefit from their group. Then I give them that new person's details (with permission) and ask them to make an introductory phone call. Now Mrs Smith enters the group and meets someone to whom she has already spoken, someone who will take her under their wing for a few weeks and introduce her to people. She need not fear that she will be ignored, or sit alone wishing she had never darkened their door. Most people remember that difficult first step into the unknown and are only too glad to be able to help.

Sometimes, a response follows one of my articles. For example, not every would-be dancer can cope with sequence dancing, the main type of dancing available. In my article and also when travelling around the groups, I asked if anyone would be interested in an afternoon disco full of music from the 50s, 60s and 70s. With help to spread the word, an afternoon disco is a real possibility.

Another couple emailed me and said they would like to help make their street friendlier. They had tried inviting people to their home but found their neighbours reluctant to return the favour. Together we decided to invite the people in their street to a coffee morning at a local café. I wrote a letter which I posted through their doors. To our delight twelve people came to the first coffee morning and a slightly different twelve joined the second one. Those who came enjoyed it so much that they asked if it could continue. In the early days, we held coffee mornings once a fortnight but after a while they decided they would like them every week. About fifteen to twenty people now meet weekly. Two skittles groups have grown from this coffee initiative, a weekly daytime one and a monthly evening one.

The café where this group meets is on a bus route. A group member discovered that the bus would be withdrawn, stranding thousands of elderly people who rely on the bus for shopping, visits to the doctor's and other amenities. I suggested to the local councillor in charge of transport that, if he were to come to our coffee morning, he could discuss the proposal with a ready-made group of residents. I put the word out and suggested that people could invite their friends and any interested parties. One hundred and fifty people arrived, forcing us to hold the meeting outside because they wouldn't fit in the café. I'm glad to be able to tell you that we did manage to save the bus!

Sometimes the spaces might look less like assets: empty buildings, plots of wasteland, shops to let... These physical buildings and spaces all have a potential for community usefulness. With the help of a full-time fundraiser who works for the project, communities have come together to transform waste ground into gardens. Our fundraiser finds and publicises information about available grants and helps people with the application. He sends the Community Builders weekly details of grants and funding for which they might bid. We then pass the details to possible community beneficiaries. There is money out there if you know where to find it.

Sometimes funding is not an issue. One group wanted to make raised flower beds on a patch of ground. Although funds were available, the people involved discovered that, between them, they had everything they needed without the extra money. One member had abundant wood he did not need. Another had topsoil left over after a building project. Others had given cuttings and plants from their gardens. The flower beds were made and filled from sharing what they had.

Currently a couple of Community Builders are working together to find premises which will host a Men in Sheds project.[1] We have about half a dozen men interested, one of whom is about to start renovating a flat. We suggested that they could start by helping him with that. It will help them to bond, removes the need for rented premises and gives that man a welcome boost to his efforts as these are all skilled men.

What has Asset Based Community Development got to do with loneliness?

The above examples show that it has the capacity to reduce loneliness in our neighbourhoods. As community members connect with each other and remember what a community is they will see that they can do something for themselves. They begin to recognise each other. One lady said to me, "Frank walks past our house every day with his dog. Before this coffee morning we didn't know him but now we stop and speak to each other." Frank is a widower. He now has people who will notice and investigate if, one day, he doesn't pass their door. That is community in action.

Research has shown that people who can name five of their neighbours feel safer in their street. ABCD is about helping to make those connections. It is about bringing people together and encouraging them to recognise that their voice counts. It helps to overcome the feeling that there is no point in doing anything.

Can you imagine what would happen if we enabled members of our churches to actively seek to make their communities stronger? We all know "connectors". All they need is the permission to go out there and do what they do best.

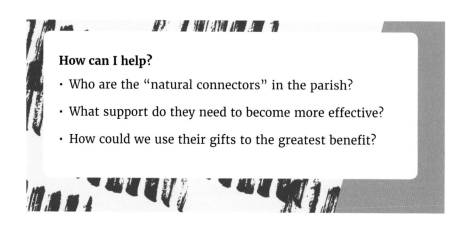

How can I help?

- Who are the "natural connectors" in the parish?

- What support do they need to become more effective?

- How could we use their gifts to the greatest benefit?

"Our human compassion binds us the one to the other – not in pity or patronisingly, but as human beings who have learnt how to turn our common suffering into hope for the future."

Nelson Mandela

Endnotes

1. The website for Men in Sheds is <http://menssheds.org.uk>, accessed 21 July 2017.

4

Loneliness within our churches

Going to a different church is a valuable experience. Holidays are a great way to do this. Seek out a church that looks friendly and see what it feels like to be the newcomer. Often we think our churches are friendly places. Because we have been there for some years and have made our friends, we have connections.

The church can feel a very different place to the newcomer who knows nobody.

We moved four hundred miles away. I was a young mum. I left a vibrant church community and many friends. I did not know how I would survive without the weekly support of the Ladies' Group which met for Bible study and prayer. Our families were over an hour away. My husband worked long hours and I was alone with two small children. I knew nobody. Life looked bleak.

Two people from the church had a tremendous impact on my life. Francine, a lady in her sixties, took me under her wing and introduced me to Maria, who had also recently moved into the area. Maria's two children were a little older than mine and already in school. Francine's and Maria's invitation to join their prayer group was an answer to my prayer.

Lyn also turned my life from awful to bearable when she quickly befriended me at the playgroup. She invited my children to her children's birthday party the week after we arrived. Then the playgroup disbanded for the summer, a mere month after my older son, Fred, had started there. I faced the prospect of three long, empty months but Lyn invited me to join a group of mums who met weekly during the summer. Lyn didn't know me. We weren't friends, but she made sure I came each week. Every Sunday she made a point of speaking to me and checking that we would come. My children were able to make friends and so was I. It made so much difference to us all.

Where are all the young people in our churches? Ask yourself: what are we providing for them? Is there a Parent and Toddler Group? Is there a playgroup or nursery? Is there somewhere for them to meet and make friends? The Ladies' Group I mentioned earlier included mums with children because one lady played with the children in an upstairs room while the rest of us enjoyed some much-needed fellowship and spiritual refreshment. In my next church, I attended a daytime prayer group because a friend from the Mums and Toddlers' Group took care of my children. When I moved to the South West, Lyn took over that role, freeing me to belong to a new prayer group. I could only belong to these prayer groups because other people stepped up and offered to help.

When we moved to the South West, I felt that this was the friendliest and most active church I had ever belonged to. There was a Mums and Tots' Group, a playgroup, Children's Liturgy on a Sunday and a good team of trained welcomers. People approached me, spoke to me and introduced me to others. I made friends and felt connected.

Six years ago, I moved church and was again a newcomer after more than twenty years in the same place. Suddenly no one knew me, hadn't watched my children grow up, didn't even know I had children. My husband is not a churchgoer and so I always go on my own although he joins me at coffee later.

In this church, people make contact with each other. You are welcomed at the entrance with a handshake, welcomed again and given a bulletin at the internal door. Someone else waits in the gallery. There are two coffee points at the back of the church. The minister encourages newcomers to go to a particular side, suggesting quicker service and you will get a nicer cup. The distinctive coffee cups are a clever technique for alerting others to new people. The congregation then takes responsibility to convert strangers into friends.

I can say from experience that this church is very good at welcoming. For a year, I sat in a different place every week, and found that whoever I sat next to made a point of speaking to me. It is hard to feel unwelcome when that happens! Within a few weeks, I was invited to help out at Messy Church.[1] After the Sunday service, one of the elders regularly made contact to see how I was settling in. I was encouraged to look at the various volunteering opportunities and make an informed decision. This was somewhere that I wanted to stay and so did a lot of other people. This inclusive church caters for all age groups and all types of people whilst always looking out to do more.

Non-churchgoing children and young people are invited to join the Girls and Boys Brigade, Youth Clubs and Youth Discipleship groups, regardless of whether or not they are Christian. Young parents are invited to Morning Out, a large and active Parent and Toddler Group. Enquirers can attend a Christianity Explored Course. There are parenting courses and a CAP Debt Centre puts on regular budgeting courses and, for several years whilst there was a need, we ran a job club. A weekly lunch for elderly people is followed by an afternoon club with a mixture of social and Christian talks. Our café sends its profits to overseas missions. All these activities demand a high level of volunteers and active membership. Through volunteering in church and our many house groups people find shared interests and friends.

We have experimented with various weekends away. These have been life-changing events for many of us. We came to know people by name, make time for conversations and share our feelings and our lives. The weekends away changed the atmosphere in our church: we "belonged" in a real way because of our time together. One woman shared that she hated church and felt terribly lonely each Sunday. However, following the weekend away, she wanted to change things for other people who felt the same way. This was the starting point for our Fresh Hope group.

Our Fresh Hope group is affiliated to Fresh Hope in America and helps people who are affected by mental health issues – their own or someone close to them. This group provides a secure, confidential drop-in space. This is a place where it is okay to be Christian and not yet be healed. Sharing personal stories helps us to calm even our most suffocating and isolating fears, leading us all to understand, empathise and feel less alone.

We also regularly ask the congregation to wear their names on a sticky label. These Sundays offer a chance to discover (and perhaps remember!) the name of the person you have been talking to for months or even years... although, these days, I just admit that I have forgotten someone's name as it usually allows them to divulge the same about me!

A very easy exercise is to make space at some point in the service for people to speak to each other. It often happens at Christmas or Easter at the sign of peace but why not try to make it more regular? The time when the children go out for Sunday school or their own liturgy is a natural break in the service when this can happen. These small activities can make the difference between welcoming the newcomer and isolating them.

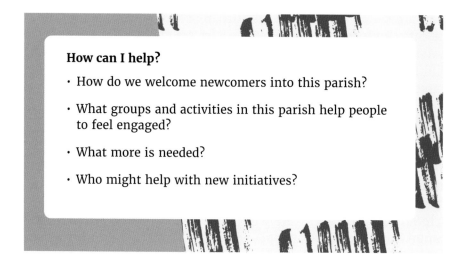

How can I help?

· How do we welcome newcomers into this parish?

· What groups and activities in this parish help people to feel engaged?

· What more is needed?

· Who might help with new initiatives?

What do we do about loneliness at Christmas?

As a big family holiday, Christmas can be one of the loneliest times of the year. Cracks widen with the pressure to look happy, to be happy. Everyone loves Christmas – don't they?

Well, the simple answer is: No, they don't. Being by yourself at Christmas is exacerbated by the fact that everyone expects you to be with your family. That is okay if you have a happy family ready to gather everyone in but often that is not the case. Thus, people on their own feel it all the more keenly.

There is a real need for us to raise awareness of loneliness at Christmas. Last Christmas, one of our local Community Christmas Day meals attracted over a hundred people! An unmarried friend of mine told me that when her mother died she had decided to volunteer at a Community Christmas meal so as not to be alone. I asked her about it afterwards and she said how much she had enjoyed being part of the team cooking and serving meals and then sitting down to eat with all the volunteers. Instead of feeling alone, she felt she was doing something to help others not to be lonely.

Some friends invite unmarried members of the congregation to join them for the Christmas Day meal. My parents always welcomed foreign students who could not afford to go home. My husband and I invite single friends to join our family Christmas celebrations. This was especially helpful to us the year that both our children were abroad and not coming home for Christmas. Rather than feel the awful "empty nest" we filled the house with people and had a great time.

Perhaps you are reading this, thinking that's okay for you but I don't have any family and my friends are all occupied with their families at Christmas. Then why not find a Christmas meal that needs volunteers? If they don't need volunteers in the kitchen they are always glad of someone who can sit at the table and help those present to relax and enjoy themselves. Book yourself in and do not feel guilty about it. You might also consider putting a message out on Next Door or Facebook, asking if anyone would like to join you for Christmas dinner at a local pub.[2] I am sure that you will not eat alone.

Give someone else a Happy Christmas!

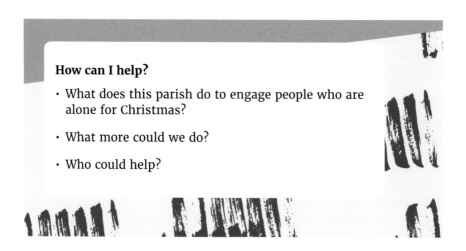

How can I help?

· What does this parish do to engage people who are alone for Christmas?

· What more could we do?

· Who could help?

Somehow, not only for Christmas
But all the long year through,
The joy that you give to others
Is the joy that comes back to you.

And the more you spend in blessing
The poor and lonely and sad,
The more of your heart's possessing
Returns to you glad.

John Greenleaf Whittier

Endnotes

1. See <https://www.messychurch.org.uk>, accessed 21 July 2017.

2. If you're not familiar with Next Door, this is the web address: <https://nextdoor.co.uk>, accessed 21 July 2017.

5

Loneliness and vulnerability

Loneliness is not just a problem at Christmas, I would like to share some information I have gleaned from some relevant TEDx talks. They were available online in 2017 as I was writing this book (see web references at the end of this chapter). I hope they will still be there for you to enjoy by the time you read this.

Loneliness is both unpleasant and an emotion that should not be ignored. In his talk entitled *The Lethality of Loneliness*, John Cacioppo gives some worrying statistics.[1] The odds for dying earlier are given as follows:

Living with air pollution	5%
Living with obesity	20%
Excessive drinking	30%
Living with loneliness	45%

Living with loneliness is more dangerous to our long-term health than excessive drinking or obesity!

In a society where we are increasingly isolated from one another, this is a problem that we need to take seriously. People do not like to admit to feeling lonely because it marks them out as a "loser". We all have witnessed the friendless child in the playground or maybe we were that child. Human beings are "pack animals": we need the company of others. As social creatures, we look out for each other. Loneliness causes our brains to snap into a self-preservation mode. The further we move from social interaction the less empathy we feel for other people.

John Cacioppo describes experiments, in which people were shown pictures of negative things, for example, a man held at gunpoint. The lonelier the brain seeing these images the less activity they saw in the area of the brain that showed empathy. A lonely person, disengaged from society, no longer looks out for the herd but goes into self-preservation mode.

What does this mean for us as individuals? Cacioppo says that just as hunger and thirst are signals that we need to eat or drink, so loneliness is a signal that we need to take action, to reconnect with the significant people in our lives. It is easy to feel that we want others to approach us and take away our loneliness but just as someone else cannot satisfy your hunger or thirst by eating on your behalf, neither can they cure your loneliness. You need to make your own connections. Find one person in whom you can confide and who can confide in you. Promote good relational connections by sharing good times with friends and family. You can promote a collective connectedness by belonging to a group. These can be people volunteering together, people who share a common interest or just a local coffee morning.

In another TEDx talk, Baya Voce usefully stresses that we all need to be seen, heard and valued.[2] We can do this by making an "anchor of connection" through a regular weekly date to meet with friends or family. She suggests that you find something you are already doing and keep doing it so that it is what you do come rain or shine. When the storms hit, you have your safe port, you don't need to seek it out. On Mondays, you meet your friends for a coffee. On Sundays, you sit down to Sunday lunch with your family. On Wednesdays, you go to your local house group. On Saturdays, you work in a charity shop. These are things that will help keep you connected so that in the tough times you will not be stranded.

> **How can I help?**
> - Why does loneliness matter?
> - Who are lonely people in this parish?
> - Why are they lonely?
> - How do we help them?
> - How could we help them?

"We have all known the long loneliness, and we have found that the answer is community."

Dorothy Day

Vulnerability and our need to share

Sometimes our loneliness is brought on by a fear of being honest with each other. What do you do when you feel you have lost your faith? To whom, among your friends of faith, do you feel you can turn?

In an ideal world, the answer would be any one of them. In the actual world, we look around and think, "I couldn't tell him: he would lose all respect for me. I can't tell her because her faith is shaky enough without seeing that I have lost mine. I could speak to her if only she weren't so busy with her elderly parents and her grandchildren. He's got far too much on his plate. She would laugh at me. He would gossip about me." We dismiss one person after another, projecting our fears onto them, talking to no one and, as a result, we fret and worry by ourselves. Our problem goes around and around our heads like a demented bluebottle trying to escape. We are trapped with our doubts and our fear that "they" might find out; that we will be seen as the hypocrite we think that we are. Sermons no longer ring true, songs ring hollow and yet, as people of faith we long for that old certainty to return. At times like these we need our friends more than ever but we are afraid of the very people who might help us.

We have just created the perfect fertile soil for loneliness to creep in and take hold. It would be so easy to give up, to stop going to church, to stop seeing our old friends. We convince ourselves that they don't care anyway or they would have noticed something was wrong. We become so good at dissembling, at making ourselves look okay, at answering, "I'm fine," rather than telling the truth... How could they know what is going on in our minds?

What can we do to get out of this vicious circle of our own making? We have to trust someone with what is going on in our heads. That someone may be an old and trusted friend or it may be an independent counsellor, secular or Christian, from outside our circle, where we can trust that what we say will go no further. Whoever we choose, we have to be totally honest with them. We can only deal with those feelings by bringing them out into the light. Such transparency makes a world of difference!

In the past two years, the deaths of people to whom I always turned in times of trouble have led to long struggles with grief, loss, anger and what I thought was an inability to pray. Attending a less conventional church service, two brave women shared their stories of times when they felt the Lord had abandoned them. In being honest with them about where I was and how I felt, in praying with them, the world looks a different place. It is okay to be angry and to rage at God: telling God how we feel is being honest with him. It is in coming before him as I am rather than as I am not, that God can help me to rediscover hope, love and security in my life, loves and relationships. To use an analogy, the greatest surgeon would find it hard to repair my broken leg if I refused to admit that it is broken, so why should a broken heart be any different?

Sharing our own fragility gives others the courage to share theirs. In our frailty we can become "wounded healers", not because we are "okay" but because we also know what it is to suffer. Our listening is authentic, arising from the lived personal understanding of the pain of loneliness, loss and bereavement. The mutual experience of loneliness means that, perhaps surprisingly, it can become an opportunity for growth, compassion, insight and empathy. It need not be an overwhelming experience of drowning with nobody to come to the rescue. Sometimes all you can do is to allow people to weep and weep with them, openly or in the silence of your heart. God does the rest. We are not called to be fixers but to be channels of love from God who is the ultimate fixer.

How can I help?

· In this parish, how do we reach out to people who feel abandoned in their grief?

· Do we offer support for those who are bereaved?

· How do we engage people who are living alone?

· What more could we do?

· Who could help?

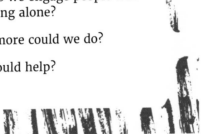

"There can be no vulnerability without risk; there can be no community without vulnerability; there can be no peace – ultimately no life – without community."

M. Scott Peck

Endnotes

1. John Cacioppo, "The Lethality of Loneliness", TED Talk at TEDxDesMoines <https://www.youtube.com/watch?v=_OhxlO3JoAO>, accessed 21 July 2017.
2. Baya Voce, "The Simple Cure for Loneliness", TEDxSaltLakeCity <https://www.youtube.com/watch?v=KSXh1YfNyVA>, accessed 21 July 2017.

6

You can change the future

As I write this we are approaching the 2017 General Election. Yesterday I cut out of one of the campaign leaflets the words "You can change the future" and stuck it on the wall by my desk. These words challenge and inspire me. I know that there are many more lonely and isolated people I need to reach and I want to make a difference to their lives.

Now I know that it is not all down to me. We each need to take responsibility for ourselves, our own thoughts, feelings and, ultimately, our own happiness. However, I can help to turn around the culture and some of the circumstances that are holding people back. If I can help my community to create welcoming meeting spaces, it will be much easier for them to overcome the fear of rejection and thereby get involved and connected with others.

So why stick the words "You can change the future" on my wall and at the head of this chapter?

What we say to ourselves, about ourselves and the internal chatter that goes on in our heads is very powerful. Joyce Meyer, in her books and television series (see www.joycemeyer.com) suggests that we can control both what we think and how we behave.[1] It should be obvious but often it isn't. We allow our thoughts to wander wherever they please and do not think of reining them in.

A psychiatric nurse suggested a very helpful and practical strategy to overcome negative thinking: catch the thought, hold it, write it down and question its veracity. In this way, you stop your thoughts from rapidly spiralling downwards. When that one negative thought is written down, you can question it. Maybe it is true. You do have cancer and it is painful and hard. Maybe the thought is not true: you have plenty of friends but you haven't connected with them lately. Writing the thought down allows us an opportunity for a truth diagnosis. In many cases our negative thoughts are not true and we need to stop the downward cycle.

What we tell ourselves about ourselves is powerful stuff. If I look in the mirror and say to myself, "You are too fat" then that is the image I will carry around with me all day. If I look in the mirror and tell myself, "You look great" then that is the image I carry. It is the same me but with totally different outcomes. I wonder if, like me, you sometimes shop for clothes and absolutely nothing looks good on you and other times everything looks good. I think it is about the image we are carrying of ourselves not what the clothes actually look like. Our bodies don't change that much from day to day but how we think about them does.

The dentist recently asked me to fill in a form that asked me to say on a scale of one to ten how I felt about my smile. I decided to ring ten. My teeth aren't beautiful, straight and pearly white like all the toothpaste adverts but it is my smile and it suits me. What a dull world it would be if we all had the same straight white teeth and pearly smile! Your smile comes from the inside and is not really about your teeth at all.

Our thoughts carry great weight and they can change us from a weak-minded, pitiful person to a strong and confident one. When I was in junior school I was shy and retiring. Nobody believes me when I tell them that now but it is true. I decided to change when I went to secondary school. I chose to go to a school where no one knew me so I was able to be anyone I wanted to be. I set out to have more confidence and to make friends. I admit I still wasn't great at making friends but I had more than before. Each time I have gone to a new place it has become easier. These days I don't think twice about starting a conversation with a complete stranger in the street, at a bus stop, in a queue... That is my job and I don't find it hard.

Various TED talks and popular psychology books carry the same message. You are what you think you are, so doesn't it make sense to think yourself into a better place? Even our body posture makes a difference. If I allow myself to slump in my chair and look as though I am feeling low then my mind will assume that must be how I am feeling. Conversely, if I sit up straight and smile, my brain recognises positive happy body posture and my feelings start to connect with my body. If I am feeling down, I can actually change that by altering my posture: my feelings will follow what my body is doing. Apparently, our brains cannot differentiate between fake and real smiles and laughter so if we smile or laugh, even when we don't feel like it, we can actually make our feelings catch up with our body!

Don't forget the old saying, "Smile and the world smiles with you." It is one very good reason to smile at strangers in the street. You can lift their day because, however they are actually feeling, most people return a smile and feel better for doing so.

Thinking points

· Am I aware of where my thoughts are taking me?

· Am I aware of my body posture?

· What does my body posture say about me to myself? To others?

· How can I use the information in this chapter to help myself? To help others?

"The best remedy for those who are afraid, lonely or unhappy is to go outside, somewhere where they can be quiet, alone with the heavens, nature and God. Because only then does one feel that all is as it should be."

Anne Frank

Endnotes

1. Joyce Meyer's DVDs and accompanying books *The Power of Words* and *Battlefield of the Mind* have influenced my thinking and the ideas in this chapter.

7

The old has gone, the new is on its way

Within the space of twenty-four months, three of my favourite "go to" people, four other friends and one very dear father-in-law died. With grief, anger and loneliness in full measure in my life, my faith took a hard hit and my favourite prayer became "Help thou my unbelief". I took the brave decision to share how I was feeling with a trusted friend.

Her answer gave me great comfort so I would like to share it with you.

> Behold the old has gone. The new has come/is coming/will come... Grief numbs the emotions, so it's hard to feel things. But that's a great thing to learn, that God is still working in us and for us despite our lack of feelings – or faith. Some never learn this.
>
> Part of your current experience is due to wisdom. What? Yup! You have great wisdom and if you have ever asked for more this time is the result... You see the truth. The truth is that even the very best of our forms of Church are not good enough for what God is doing now. Even the very best. Our best intentions, programmes, organisations, charismatic-led churches, traditional ways of doing things (whether that tradition is two millennia or two decades old), are all an "old crop" – not this year's.
>
> When the farmers harvest the barley here they drill the new crop into the earth with the same machine. Currently the fields all look ploughed and barren as the harvest is over and the crops gone. But they are harbouring, deep in the earth, the new life of a completely different crop, one that will refresh the earth with all the necessary nutrients which the barley used up in its growing; one that will have its own spectacular growth period and harvest once the sun comes in the spring.
>
> Some people are going to be surprised. They are polishing their combines in readiness for barley again, but God has sown peas, or sunflowers, or potatoes, or maize or shining fields of

oilseed. Perhaps there will be something completely new, that few will recognise at first because it's been so long since that crop grew here.

You are seeing that what we have will no longer do. We need the thing God is doing... the new thing... the God-planned and executed thing. Something new.

I found this incredibly reassuring. This desert time of grief, loneliness and lack of faith can also be a time for fertilising the soil, sowing new seed and getting on board with the new plan.

So often, it is the hardest parts of our lives that will bear fruit in due season. We don't want or like these desert times. Often, we have to just trudge through them but if we can cling to the truth that God makes all things new – even this – even our grief – even our loneliness and isolation – then maybe we can eventually reach a place where we can let God pour his grace and love into our lives and allow him space to make something new out of us.

Like a snake shedding its old skin in order to grow, we too, can shed this skin of loneliness and isolation. We can put the skin somewhere safe to use as a blanket to cover someone else in their loneliness.

Walk with people in their grief and loneliness.

Listen to them.

Be with them.

"Don't walk in front of me – I may not follow;
don't walk behind – I may not lead;
walk beside me and just be my friend."

Albert Camus

But now thus says the Lord,
  he who created you, O Jacob,
  he who formed you, O Israel:
Do not fear, for I have redeemed you;
  I have called you by name, you are mine.
When you pass through the waters, I will be with you;
  and through the rivers, they shall not overwhelm you;
when you walk through fire you shall not be burned,
  and the flame shall not consume you.
For I am the Lord your God,
  the Holy One of Israel, your Saviour.
I give Egypt as your ransom,
  Ethiopia and Seba in exchange for you.

(Isaiah 43:1–3)

Desert times – recognising them and helping others

· Have I experienced any desert times in my faith walk?

· What did I learn?

· Can I access it to help myself and others in new desert times?

· Am I open to seeing God doing something new in my life or the lives of others?

8

Prayer

Praying when you feel overburdened

"I want to ask the Lord for the grace to relinquish to him, all that I feel responsible for, so I can rest in his hand totally secure and give up feeling I have to solve everything for everybody."

I wrote this prayer in my prayer journal at the start of a silent retreat in 2004. At that time I was an adult tutor, also responsible for co-ordinating a team of other tutors. I shared this role with my colleague and friend who was absent from work due to sickness. I drew a little cartoon of myself with a milkmaid's yoke, laden with heavy bags which I had labelled with all my concerns of that moment. Some were work-related, others were home-related. To one side I added a smiley face saying, "Come to me all you who are heavy laden and I will give you rest."

Jesus says, "Come to me, all you that are weary and are carrying heavy burdens, and I will give you rest... my yoke is easy, and my burden is light" (Matthew 11:28-30). In John 14:1 he says: "Do not let your hearts be troubled. Believe in God, believe also in me." Jesus asks us to trust in God and to trust in him.

It is hard to do this while we still feel that we are responsible for everybody else. That is why I love the profound wisdom of the Serenity Prayer, which comes down to accepting the stuff you can't change, changing the things you can and, best of all, recognising the difference.

You will not be able to do much for some people. Their situation is beyond your personal capability. For others, you may be able to do something. One thing is sure, for all of them you can be there, listening respectfully to their stories and granting them visibility in a world where they may well feel ignored and unseen. Do not dismiss this listening role as unimportant. Often it does far more good than you will ever know or imagine.

In the same way as you can be there for your friends, family and co-workers, Jesus is there for you. He is waiting to one side of the picture. All you have to do is call and he is there.

A life of faith means embracing times of loneliness and doubt as well as times of great belief. I found in my prayer journal these words:

> "In our emptiest spaces God has the most room to live and move and work miracles."

Times of doubt are very lonely for a Christian. It is hard to share such things especially if you are the one who usually lifts other people's faith. I have found that when others have been honest and open and made themselves vulnerable, it has allowed me to do the same. This transparency truly connects us to other people and makes a difference in their lives and ours.

Allow people to be open and honest without trying to "put them right" or "fix" them. It is not our place to judge or condemn. We need to be trustworthy custodians of people's stories.

> "God grant me the serenity
> to accept the things I cannot change;
> courage to change the things I can;
> and wisdom to know the difference."
>
> *Reinhold Niebuhr*

Different ways of praying

I touched on praying as you can and not as you can't in the previous section. Now, I would like to share some forms of prayer to do alone or with others that you may find helpful. Some people find praying aloud spontaneously comes easily. If it is your gift use it sensitively and try to discern when it is right to offer to pray in this way and when it may not be.

- **Pray as you can, not as you can't**

There are times when it is hard to pray. Remember that prayer is simply you and God together. You can do this any time, any place and in any way. So, give yourself permission to pray as you can, not as you can't. This might mean simply going for a walk or sitting in a beautiful place and allowing God to comfort you with the sights and sounds of the natural world.

- **Traditional prayers**

Some people find great comfort in familiar, traditional prayers which, when prayed together, put everyone on an equal footing and places people in a safe and known context.

- **Lectio Divina**

There is a form of scriptural prayer known as Lectio Divina, "Divine Reading". Alone or in a group, slowly read and savour a passage from scripture. At the end of the reading those present simply say whichever word or phrase resonated with them. No explanation is asked for or given of why it resonates. This can be tremendously powerful, especially if the participants go away and ponder the word or phrase that rang true for them. It can help them gain valuable insights.

- **Write a letter to God**

Somehow, putting words on paper helps us to be just one step removed from our hurt.

It is okay to be angry with God, who is big enough to handle our rages. Sometimes, like a frustrated toddler, we need to rant, rave and throw a tantrum until we have released all that pent-up emotion. Once we have done that we are able to come back into our right mind. Then we know that God is waiting for us, loving us, ready to let us reconnect with him on our own terms. What a glorious thing to know!

· Walk with the Lord

If it feels impossible to sit still and pray, walking can be freeing, getting rid of excess energy. Walk and talk to the Lord. Find a beautiful destination to sit and allow the Lord to refresh you in mind and spirit.

· Ring the changes

Another version of this is to take a verse of scripture, for example, Philippians 4:13, and read it aloud, changing the emphasis each time.

"I can do all things through Christ who strengthens me."[1]

Every word carries a different power and perspective. One day I might need the power that comes with **I**; another day it helps to know that there is **nothing** I cannot do (I can do **all things**). On another occasion, I yearn for Christ to **strengthen** me. When I feel weak and scared, it helps to know that **Christ** is my source of strength.

· The Psalms

The Psalms can bring great comfort, particularly if someone is angry and hurting. The psalmist calls out to God in frustration, despair and hopelessness. Yet at the end, having been brutally honest about his situation, the psalmist turns back to God with words of trust, praise and thanksgiving. The Psalms show us what it is to be human with the whole gamut of feelings – bad as well as good. God's grace helps us to return to a place where we can recognise and accept his mercy and forgiveness.

· Creative prayer

The list of creative ways is endless. Putting "creative prayer ideas" into Google reveals almost fifteen million results in less than a second! Why not try some of them?

There are many ways of using creative prayer and include such diverse ideas as using coloured pencils to scribble on paper, taking a psalm and illustrating it, taking a verse and writing it with calligraphic pens, weaving, embroidery, knitting, ironing, washing up, pottery, gardening, walking, meditating.

There is no right or wrong way. Prayer is a living communication with God and that is the only thing that matters. How you communicate is up to you.

- **Imaginative prayer**

Try reflecting upon a piece of scripture in which you are present in the scene either as one of the main protagonists or on the edge as an observer in the crowd.

Take, for example, when Jesus washed his disciples' feet at the Last Supper (John 13:1-17) and see yourself as one of the disciples whose feet Jesus holds in his hands and washes. Recognise that, although you are helping to support others, he is supporting you.

Take another example in which the Gospel shows how Jesus helped lonely people and gave us an example to follow.

- **Jesus and the woman at the well** (John 4:1-25)

One day Jesus is walking through a town in Samaria. He is the foreigner here. He is tired, hungry and thirsty. He sends his friends off to buy food while he rests at the well. While at the well he meets a Samaritan woman and asks her for a drink.

This amazes the Samaritan woman. Jesus is thwarting all sorts of conventions.

- Men don't speak to women.

- Jews don't speak to Samaritans.

- Jews certainly don't want to drink from the same cup as a Samaritan.

It is noon. Jesus says the woman has been married five times and the man she is now with is not her husband. This woman has to be lonely. Only someone with no friends and no chance of a friendly reception would go to the well in the heat of the day, a time when most people retire to the coolest spot they can find.

The fact that Jesus breaks the conventions enables this woman to have the feisty exchange we see. She queries why he, a Jew, would ask her, a Samaritan, for water. She does not just bow her head and give him what he asks for. Instead, she looks him in the eye and demands answers. She is not afraid of him. To be honest, she is not very pleasant to him at first. But his exchanges with her bring her to a place where she believes what he has to say and then runs back to the town to tell them who she has met.

Where did that courage come from? This is the same woman who moments before was too afraid to come and draw water with the other women of the village. Suddenly she is the bearer of good news and doesn't think twice about approaching others with it.

What does Jesus do?

- He accepts her as she is.
- He is humble enough to ask her for something she has.
- They have a two-way conversation.

When we visit someone who is lonely, we do so knowing that we do not have all the answers. We do not go in as someone who is better than them. They need us to hear their story and to walk with them in their loneliness. As we treat them with respect, as we listen without judging, we will see a change happen. Listen to the Holy Spirit to know when the time is right to offer to pray for them or with them.

How does it work?

Read the scripture passage in whatever version you have available and try to imagine the scene so it becomes real to you. Put yourself in the story and ask questions. The questions below are merely prompts which you can use or ignore as is appropriate for you. You are looking for what Jesus has to say to you through this encounter.

Let's use the same scripture of Jesus meeting with the woman at the well. Put yourself into the story.

Maybe you are Jesus. What do you see when you meet this woman? What is she like? Is she hot, tired, angry? How do you feel?

You ask for water. It is the heat of the day. Your disciples have gone off in search of food.

Do you have an ulterior motive when you ask that for water? Or do you respond to a flow of the Holy Spirit, prompting further comments and questions?

Maybe you are the woman. How do you feel when you see a man at the well? He is Jewish and you are Samaritan? What goes through your mind? What gives you the courage to answer back? What makes you see things differently? What do you think of this man at the start of your exchange? How does that change by the end of your conversation? What convinces you so much that you are prepared to run back to the village? How do you feel when the disciples approach? Do you even notice them?

Maybe you are a disciple. How do you feel about leaving Jesus to find food? How do you feel when you come back and see him talking to a woman? How do you feel when you realise she is a Samaritan? What do you make of her running off?

· **Transforming the desert** (Isaiah 41:17–20)
This gives hope where there was none. It talks of deserts being transformed.

Try immersing yourself in this passage. Read each line slowly out loud and let what it is saying resonate with your spirit. Picture yourself as the barren land being watered and refreshed.

When people are finding it difficult to pray themselves, they may like you to pray for them. In fact, even among non-believers, people are rarely upset by an offer of prayer for their intentions.

How can I help?

Who cares for the carers in this parish?

How do people let us know that they want us to pray for them?

Could we do more to support people who feel in need of prayer support?

"Prayer is the most concrete way to make our home in God."

Henri Nouwen

Endnotes

1. Scripture passage from the New King James Version®. Copyright © 1982 by Thomas Nelson. Used by permission. All rights reserved.

9

True stories

The brief for this book was to write something that could be used by pastoral workers to aid their understanding of loneliness as well as being something that they might give to anyone dealing with loneliness in their daily lives. To this end I asked people of my acquaintance, whom I knew had dealt with loneliness in their lives, if they would share something of their life stories. I have changed the names to maintain their anonymity.

I am enormously grateful to these lovely warm-hearted people for their generosity of spirit and honest reflections. I hope you will find a story which resonates with yours.

Gerard's story

Loneliness or "Just Alone"? There is a great difference

Loneliness can affect people of all ages, but it is very subjective. It is generally linked to being isolated and lack of companionship. When I was thirteen my parents separated and my older brother was at work, so I was alone for most of the time, but I do not remember ever feeling lonely or isolated. Was it because I was looking forward to life with exams and work?

Now that my wife has died after fifty-five years of marriage and after travelling the world on business, often on my own in very isolated areas, never feeling lonely, the situation is very different.

I always said that I was happy in my own skin, but how wrong I was.

I didn't realise that the awareness of my wife and the regular telephone contact made such a difference.

When we retired we had an active life together, dancing, playing bridge, walking, holidays, and so on, and many other separate activities.

So, what changed? My wife died and my purpose and motivation in life died with her. I no longer had any reason to do anything for myself, what was the point? We had three children, nine grandchildren, two great-grandchildren and in addition we had an "unofficially adopted" son with three more grandchildren. Also, I thought at the time, many friends.

After the funeral, nobody knocked at the door, nobody telephoned or emailed and very few sent texts. Life came to a grinding halt. People "didn't know what to say"!

The first thing I did was to order Sky Sports, but after a short time I realised that this didn't help and so I looked for something else to do. I came across an "Ageing Well" project called "Circles of Support", which helped people caring for a family member. I volunteered for this and, having promised to do something, I always carry it out. It takes up a minimum of nine hours and three afternoons a week.

However, although this, with other activities such as playing bridge, took up a great deal of time, it is amazing how much time there still is on your own and still nobody knocks at the door and I still have very few phone calls or texts.

So, am I lonely? I would say not, but I am very alone. I drive, so I am not isolated and I meet with people most days, so it would appear that I don't lack companionship. But all this still leaves a huge void in my life when I am alone.

For the first time in my life I understand why someone would commit suicide. Not that I am contemplating it, but this came up in a discussion with a lady who recently lost her husband and she admitted to me that she had considered it. Is this due to loneliness, depression or just grief?

So, what is the answer? I don't know, is the simple response. I am confused as to what my wife and I did together that occupied me and gave me the incentive to live.

I am capable of cooking and cleaning. I have a good pension which leaves me with no financial worries.

I have talked with people who have recently lost their wives or husbands and we all feel the same. One comment was that "he hadn't anyone to share memories with", a very interesting observation as

I have no interest in going on holiday for exactly the same reason: I see no point in visiting interesting places on my own.

The only answer it seems to me is to have someone living with me, but after fifty-five years of marriage it would feel like I was cheating on my wife. She is still alive in my mind and I talk to her every day: the difference is that she doesn't answer me!

Andrea's story

My journey with loneliness started as a child, although I couldn't name it then. Fear and shame deepened my loneliness throughout my life. This made relationships difficult. I had no sense of myself. I was what/who those around me said I was. I would change my behaviour and opinions depending on who I was with and what I thought would please them or they wanted to hear. I mostly kept quiet for fear of getting it wrong. I found it impossible to be truthful, always feeling I had to hide who I really was – not that I really knew what that was but just had an overwhelming sense of being bad.

As I grew up I was able, for a while, to bury these feelings and live what appeared to be a happy and fulfilled life. It didn't stay buried for long. Becoming a mother triggered it again and deepened my sense of fear at being "found out". If I said I wasn't coping I would be letting people down, but what I was really doing was letting my husband and children down. I withdrew and isolated myself emotionally. I hated myself and the fear and shame I felt shut out those close to me. I didn't know, nor could I name, what was happening to me. I felt so crippled by these feelings and thoughts, I was unable to ask for help – it risked me being found out and I would lose those closest to me.

Because I couldn't love myself, it greatly affected those around me. I was unable to love them and be there for them as I needed to be and so they felt unloved, unwanted and found their solace elsewhere. My husband had no idea what was going on inside of me, he just felt unloved. My divorce broke me in pieces and it has taken over twenty years for me to finally be comfortable in my own skin.

The Lord has painstakingly put me back together and still is doing so. He gave me friends who have walked beside me every step of the way:

counsellors who have helped me to value who I am; peers who have trod the same path, who knew without having to say a word. My journey of loneliness is teaching me that I am loved unconditionally, warts and all (there are plenty) by the Lord, who died for me to take away my sin and shame.

I am still travelling this road out of loneliness but he is beside me in my darkest moments. I now live in the light of Christ. He has used my friends and family and sometimes complete strangers, to show me the way to living my life, loving myself as I should and enabling me to love others as he would want me to. Loneliness and I still meet occasionally but it no longer has a hold on me and I no longer believe what it tries to tell me.

Molly's story

I feel the first time I really experienced loneliness was when my husband died. He had been ill with Alzheimer's for thirteen years.

Although he had to go into a nursing home because of his aggression towards me and also because he might harm himself, I was always there for him. I visited every day, talking to him, giving him his lunch and staying for his afternoon tea. I didn't know I was lonely until it got to a stage when my husband couldn't communicate with me any more. He lost his speech, couldn't walk and there was no recognition in his eyes. I still visited him every day. When I returned home from my visit it felt empty, although everything was still as it had been before he left.

Six months after my husband died I decided to book a holiday on my own. I decided to go to Canada. (We were going to do this trip many years previously but hadn't made it.)

It was the best thing I could have done for "me". I met a lot of nice people in the same situation as myself. After a wonderful holiday, I came back ready to face the future whatever it might be.

I have also gone back to my group called the "U3A" and, through "Ageing Well", also meet with old friends and new. I now have something to live for. I'm also hoping to go off on another holiday on my own.

Cathy's story

When you lose a loving spouse or partner to ill health, even when it is expected, the reality of loneliness makes a huge impact.

You paint on a smile, take comfort from family and friends if you have them, and try to keep yourself busy and distracted, which helps some of the time, but you feel lonely.

You have to make important decisions by yourself now and it is lonely.

You could once discuss all problems together and come up with solutions, but now it is down to you and you feel lonely. It is very daunting.

Even in the throng of a happy family occasion you can still feel so alone.

Maybe, given time, this feeling of loneliness will ease. Perhaps if you keep smiling, keep busy, help others, time will help to heal this feeling of loneliness.

There are many others around you in similar situations. Try new things, join in, mix with others and maybe, in time, loneliness can be overcome.

Elaine's story

The many faces of loneliness

There are many times in my life when I would have considered myself lonely:

As a child, I witnessed things I never should have. I protected my younger brother when these things were happening. I would keep him upstairs and out of the way of things he didn't need to hear or see. This in itself made me feel lonely because I didn't feel part of a calm family at that time. The loneliness felt worse because I didn't know who to talk to; I wanted to be loyal within the family but it was too big a burden to bear. So, I threw myself into my school studies and learnt of an inner world where I could control my world to enable me to "succeed at life", whatever that meant. This taught me to be self-reliant but at times to an unhealthy level. The saving grace for me at that point was, first, that I became a Christian at the age of fifteen and, secondly, that it fuelled my creativity: I wrote journals, poems and joined a movement at the time called "Mass Observation", a project that recorded the views of the population at that time. We would write essays on given topics and one of my pieces was once quoted on radio!

As a late teenager, I went to university and that taught me a whole new understanding of loneliness: I was away from familiarity and that was extremely difficult for me. Time away at university is perceived to be "the time of your life" but it wasn't for me or for others. I was in Loughborough, inland, flat and industrial. I mourned the loss of the sea, the rolling hills, the red soil and the sound of seagulls, tractors and familiar family and friends. This loss was eased by joining the Christian Union at the university and serving on the committee. I also made lifelong friends.

In my early twenties, I did what you should never do – moved to another part of the country, started working fulltime, married, bought my first home – all within five weeks of graduating. This was a particularly lonely time with so many changes and, once again, a sense of unfamiliarity which was, at times, debilitating. Yet through all this I matured as a person, learning to build my self-confidence and creativity. I discovered I could do calligraphy – a modern form – and left my council job to set up my own business.

When I was thirty, my husband and I were sent overseas as missionaries to Hungary, where I lived for seven years, five of them alone in a foreign country. We had someone living with us, like a daughter – someone we had known since she was eleven. But it was not to be and my husband decided to marry her. This was a level of loneliness that I would never have thought possible. I was thrown out. I saw nobody from Friday through to Monday unless I went to the church meeting, where I was perceived as a threat: young, single, female, foreign. What a recipe for isolation! Through these dark, lonely times, I learnt much about myself but even more about a faithful loving heavenly Father. Just as Joseph experienced in the Bible, periods of solitary confinement can transform someone. God often felt close, but, sometimes, he seemed very far away.

At thirty-eight, having also lived a year in a basement of a friend's home in Germany I returned to England, to my home town, when all other doors closed on me. This was also deeply isolating and lonely. I lived among boxes in my mum's home. After securing a housing association placement I was first diagnosed with moderate depression, which disallowed work for eighteen months, and then, secondly, with a rare form of breast cancer. While the cancer disappeared after chemotherapy, I still lost my hair, married again two weeks later wearing a wig, and am still on treatment seven years later. Illness, fatigue, confronting your own mortality – all make you feel lonely.

Most recently, after three years of severe ill health, mum left us to be with Jesus. So now I know a different loneliness. I've lost someone whom I loved very dearly, saw almost daily, spoke to every day; I held her hand at the end... I've lost one of my best friends. We talked about anything and everything so her loss makes me lonely inside, despite now having many new good friends and family.

How to face loneliness

The most important lesson that life has taught me is that I do not want to be a victim of circumstances or of poor personal choices. Life itself is a gift and there is always a reason to be thankful even if our finite minds find it hard to see. Everybody dies. People get sick. Relationships fail. I have experienced domestic abuse, rejection, life-threatening conditions... What have you faced? We all have a list.

Two things. Firstly, when I hid in a friend's home after being thrown out of my marriage home, her husband was like a father to me. I used to come in from work feeling traumatised by another day of teaching, running to the toilets to throw up and then back to the classroom to teach again... He always refused to speak to me until I had eaten a healthy meal, had drunk enough fluids and had slept. He knew that these three essential self-care tools would help me to feel and think differently. He was right. I felt better and I was able to think more clearly and accurately about my situation.

Secondly, beware! The thief comes only to steal and kill and destroy. But God has come that we may have life and have it to the full! (John 10:10). Choose the latter!

Susan's story

My fisherman husband drowned at sea at the age of forty-six. He left for work before I woke that morning and, surprisingly, wasn't already at home when I returned from work with the children that evening. Unknown to me he was already deemed to be lost at sea and an official search was already under way. His body was eventually recovered from the sea at about 11pm. My daughters were ten and sixteen years old at the time.

My memories of those first few days are almost non-existent. His body had to be formally identified but I chose not to see him again. Lots of family, especially his family, visited us. There were decisions to be made about a funeral, visits to the bank, marine accident investigation, inquest, visit from the fishermen's mission... So much to sort out.

My job involved working in the community. News of his death was all over the local newspapers, television and eventually national press. I decided to take a break from work, as the prospect of talking about his death to my clients was something that I couldn't bear thinking about. (I was eventually off work for over two-and-a-half years.)

I tried to avoid meeting anyone who would know what happened. I stopped going to my local shop and I started doing my weekly shop in the next town, just in case I met someone who might know.

I received messages from people I had not heard from in a long time, inviting me for coffee and so on. I didn't respond to any of them.

The feeling of emptiness is totally overwhelming. My husband's brother had died a couple of years before him and I found spending time with his widow the easiest for me. She was very angry at the death of her husband from cancer after only four years of marriage. (She is still angry seven years since he died.)

I didn't seek any sort of medical help or counselling as I just didn't want to talk to anyone about how I felt, knowing that I needed to be strong for my girls, for his parents and for my elderly parents. I tended to stay at home on my own as much as I could.

My relief from this was when both daughters ended up in hospital within a week of each other. Due to my daughters' injuries, many hours were spent at the local hospital – sometimes a couple of times a week – and this lasted for eighteen months. My parents were both also hospitalised, with me needing to spend even more time visiting the hospital. I came to realise that it was possible to chat to new people who knew nothing about my husband's death. I eventually became a hospital volunteer, something I thoroughly enjoy. I went back to work part-time. The first time I set foot in a patient's house, almost the first thing she asked me was "How is your husband? He's a fisherman, isn't he?" I explained that he had passed away, news which upset her. Afterwards I turned to my boss and said, "And that's why I gave up work! Just the situation I wanted to avoid!"

Although I enjoy life generally, I still hate my own company, cry at songs that come on the radio (it always seems to happen in the car!). Some days I relive the emotions of what happened the night he died.

I feel like the odd one out if I go out with friends who are couples but I am not sure that I am interested in being in another relationship. I don't relish the thought of being on my own as I get older, but am enjoying the freedom of being my own person. I'm not sure I can fall in love with someone new when I still love my late husband.

10

Some poems from the heart about loneliness

Sometimes it is easier to put into verse what is going on in our lives and heads and hearts. The poems that follow are written from the heart and give a glimpse into loneliness at different times in our lives.

I am indebted to Carol Pallett, and to my friend who prefers to remain anonymous, for sharing their poetry with us.

Endless Silence
by Carol Pallett

I believe "Silence" is a noise you can hear
It appears endless and becomes full of fear

It can cut right through you like a knife
And for many long hours fill your life

It takes many prisoners of any age
And I can list many reasons to fill my page

You switch on the TV and the radio
As more endless hours come and go

You can count every second, of every minute, of every day,
Whose painful loneliness won't go away

You pray for someone to come along
And fill your hours with words or song

You pray for a neighbour to ask you in for a cup of tea
But you know from experience, that will never be!

If someone died in these houses,
would anyone know?
As the 4x4s, they come and go!

They drive right past me at such great speed
As my walking down this long, long street,
they pay me no heed.
They've places to go, and people to see –
And conversations to have –
that don't include me!

The telephone is silent,
It used to ring off the wall
But no one can spare a minute to give me a call
I miss all the gossip
And the chats without care.
My diary is empty
Because no one's left out there!

Another Day

by Carol Pallett

I get up in the morning
And I stop and stare
At the empty side of the bed
With no one there

I turn on the radio to fill the air with sound
My only company today that can be found!

I can see no reason to get up and get dressed
It's been a long time since anyone has
seen me looking my best!

I gave up the cake baking
Hoping someone would call
I retrieved one letter from down the hall
Now no one writes with paper and pen
Looking forward with enjoyment
as I once did then

As I walk down the path to the end of the drive
Does anyone live down this street?
Is there anyone actually alive?
They are busy, busy, busy as can be
With never time for me or tea!

You close the curtains, as night draws in
And you throw another uneaten dinner
into the bin
Somehow you don't fancy it today
It would be wonderful to share a meal some day

As darkness descends –
You climb into bed and close your eyes
And you lay there silently,
waiting for another sunrise.

Poem written in a time of grief
(Anonymous)

Oh, my friends, my friends
Where were you all?
Could you not guess that I needed a call?
Was it so much to want?
Too hard for you to do?
Pick up the phone
Speak words kind and true?

Yes, I know you were praying
I know you were there
But it wasn't enough
To show me you care.
I felt alone,
Deserted
In my hour of need
And now

That memory makes my heart bleed
And I rant and I rave inside my head
Till my heart is bursting with
Anger instead.

So now when you call
I want to rant and to scream
It's too late
Far too late
You have shattered my dream
Where were you all?
I just needed a call

Don't tell me
"I love you"
If you won't act
Don't tell me you care
If you won't be there
You let me alone
In the quiet of the night
You left me to bear
My grief
Out of your sight

I can't bear that you did that
And you think you're my friends
I watched with my poor dad
Right to the end
But where were you all
When I needed my friends?

Now I'm lost and alone
And angry with you
So angry, so angry, so angry
It's true
My grief, my relief
And my anger at you.

We stand on rock
(**Anonymous**)

We stand
On rock
You and I
Carved from
a single
Piece
I cannot
Escape
Your Embrace.
There is
Tension
Struggle
And yet
I know
I could
So easily
Lean in
To Your
Soft
Embrace
You will not
Let me go
And I do not
Want you to
I am held
Safe
Despite
Protests
Here we
Stand
Struggle
Then
Peace

Faith is not faith
Where there is
No doubt

Web resources

Alongside the web references listed at the end of relevant chapters, you may find the following organisations and their websites of use. (Web references below accessed 24 July 2017.)

Age UK

<http://www.ageuk.org.uk> Charity working to make life better for older people.

Beginning Experience

<http://www.beginningexperience.org> Serving the widowed, separated and divorced.

Cruse Bereavement Care

<https://www.cruse.org.uk> Bereavement counselling service.

Samaritans

<https://www.samaritans.org> Secular listening service run by trained volunteers. Call Free: 116 123 anytime day or night.

The Silver Line

<https://www.thesilverline.org.uk> Information, friendship, advice and help for older people. Call: 0800 4 70 80 90 anytime day or night.